Old AIRDRIE

by

CAMPBELL McCUTCHEON

South Bridge Street circa 1907

LANARKSHIRE HERITAGE SERIES

VIGILANTIBUS

AIRDRIE.

HERALDIC SERIES.

INTRODUCTION

This part of the Monklands has been inhabited for thousands of years but the first real evidence of civilisation is a Roman coin found in the garden of one of the houses in Aitchison Street. The old Roman Road from the south must have run through the town on its way from Motherwell to the Antonine Wall and its network of forts and settlements. The first record of Airdrie though is probably the battle of Arderyth in AD577. This battle culminated in Rydderech the Bountiful defeating Aidan the Perfidious and the securing of the independence of Strathclyde. Merlin, the great Caledonian poet, was given a golden torc (Celtic necklace) for his verses about this glorious event, even though he was on the losing side.

The first definite written mention of the area is in the 14th Century when Airdrie justified a small mention in the Register of the Great Seal in 1373. The settlement was to remain as a small group of a few cottages for over 300 years. In 1695 Airdrie became a market town. Four annual fairs complemented the weekly market and the hamlet began, slowly, to grow in size. The population of, maybe, 250 were engaged in weaving, distilling, brewing and candle making. The landscape around the town was inhospitable and the winds were broken only by a few remaining trees from the once great Caledonian Forest. Those parts that weren't covered by trees were peaty boglands.

The town grew and expanded, mainly as a centre for hand loom weaving. For a long time this was the staple industry of many parts of west Scotland, but by the beginning of the 19th Century this trade was beginning to decline in some areas. There were two main causes of this, one being the advent of new power looms and associated spinning machinery and the other the ending of the Napoleonic War. The hand loom industry had boomed throughout this long war. Uniforms, blankets and tents all had to be manufactured for the troops and when the war ended there was a great depression in Britain. By 1819 there was great unrest amongst the weavers. Many had lost their extremely well paid jobs and others had had to take massive cuts in wages. In 1820 there was an uprising against the unpopular government. It was partly Government inspired as a way of getting rid of the political agitators and, as a consequence, the Government came down hard on the Radicals. After a small skirmish at Bonnymuir (the Radicals were on their way to Falkirk to capture the munitions kept at Carron Company) many of the troublemakers were caught. Three were hanged at Stirling and others were transported to Australia. The end of hand loom weaving was near.

By the 1830s a new industry had become established. Coal had been found in the Monklands in the 12th or 13th Century, but a viable trade hadn't begun until the Monkland Canal was built. By the 1830s Coatbridge was a hive of activity with blast furnaces producing thousands of tons of iron yearly. Most of the coal and ironstone was mined in New Monkland and mining became the staple industry. The coal mines attracted engineering firms and the town began to grow rapidly. By 1841 the population of the town was approaching 12,500 and it was to grow to nearly 20,000 by the turn of the century. The influx of population caused a boom in house building, but most of these new houses were thrown up with little regard for those who had to stay in them. Housing conditions for the working classes were horrendous and there was overcrowding, dirt and disease everywhere. Many tried to forget their wretched lifestyles by drinking themselves into oblivious stupor in the town's numerous pubs. At one point there was a pub for every 169 inhabitants of the town – and they all did a roaring trade.

The decline came after the First World War. Coal mining was already in serious decline, but in the great depression 50% of the adult population was out of work. Meantime the town was growing out the way. Over 3000 local authority houses were built in the inter-war years and many of the slums were demolished. The Second World War gave the town a boost and put many of the unemployed back into work. Afterwards Airdrie began its regeneration. Boots the Chemist came to the town in 1949 and new industry began to grow along the route of the new A8 (repeating a process begun in 1797 when the Kings Highway was opened between Glasgow and Edinburgh).

While the old established industries that made Airdrie famous the world over have gone, new ones have taken their place. In the 1950s Pye came to the town and other electronics firms followed into the area. House building continued as the town rid itself of its legacy of poor housing and it became a dormitory settlement for Glasgow and Cumbernauld. In 1993 Airdrie successfully held the National Mod and the local authority has ploughed money into the area in an attempt to make a better environment for Airdrieonians. After a long period of decline the town is now going from strength to strength.

3

The Imperial Tube Works were constructed between 1898 and 1900. Over 1000 employees worked on the 40 acre site which was owned by Stewarts & Lloyds. During the First World War much of the production was turned over to munitions. Shells and guns were the works' main output. During the Second World War, demand was again for munitions, but the works also produced nitrogen cylinders for aircraft as well as pipes for PLUTO (a large pipeline from England to France) which kept our troops supplied with fuel during, and after, the D-Day invasion.

Airdrie House, Airdrie.

Airdrie House was originally the home of the Hamiltons of Airdrie and later became the residence of Sir John Wilson. He provided the land for the town's west end parks as well as the Town Hall. Airdrie House was the district's Maternity Hospital for many years, serving both Airdrie and Coatbridge and first opening as such in August 1919. It was demolished in 1964, after having stood empty for two years. In 1971, work began on a new hospital on the site, the Monklands District General Hospital, which opened in 1977.

The Gushet house stood at the junction of Alexander Street and Aitchison Street and was demolished in 1937. Road improvements in this area have widened the roads and provided much open space. This early Edwardian view is taken from around where the War Memorial stands.

West End Park was laid out between 1909 and 1913. The South Burn, which now runs about four feet underneath the park, was culverted and the ravine between Alexander Street and the railway was used as a coup and filled in. The Linlee Bridge originally crossed the South Burn at Alexander Street just about where the War Memorial is nowadays. Sir John Wilson, who lived across the road in Airdrie House, provided the money to pay for the cost of laying out the paths and flower beds.

Alexander Street was named after one of the earlier residents of Airdrie House. This part of town was developed after the turnpike road from Edinburgh to Glasgow was completed in 1797. Travel to and from the town became easier and Glasgow could be reached in only an hour and ten minutes by the new stage coaches. The stage coaches had names such as "Red Rover", "Being Up" and "Royal Telegraph" and were hauled by four horses. Six passengers could sit inside and twelve were accommodated outside. Previous to the opening of the turnpike it took over a day to traverse the forty of so miles between Edinburgh and Glasgow.

Andrew Stirling, of Drumpellier, purchased a chunk of land in this part of town, which at the turn of the 19th century was still cultivated, and started building here. He provided the Airdrie Inn at the Cross as well as numerous other buildings along Stirling Street. This view, looking to Stirling Street from Alexander Street, has changed little. The two buildings on the extreme left have been demolished and their site is now used as a tyre and exhaust centre.

STIRLING STREET, AIRDRIE

D 2917

Many of the buildings in this late 1950s view of Stirling Street still remain today. Cleveland petrol has disappeared from our garage forecourts although the garage on the right is still there. The building just next to what is now the 'Kall-Kwik Copy Centre' had just been demolished when this photo was taken and the tram lines still hadn't been removed either. This must have caused problems for the few cars on the road then. Tram-lining was always one of the hazards of driving in town. Sometimes, the car's wheels would get trapped in the tram lines and no amount of turning the steering wheel would release the car from the rails.

THE PUBLIC BATHS AND TOWN HALL, AIRDRIE   D 6444

The Public Baths were opened in October 1935 and included a large laundry as well as a gymnasium. The pool is 75 feet by 35 feet. Next to it is the Sir John Wilson Town Hall which opened in 1912. Nowadays it is impossible to park outside the front due to the sheer volume of traffic that now hurtles along Stirling Street. Back in the 1950s there were fewer cars on the road and the owners of the Triumph Mayflower and Austin A55 estate car certainly had it so much better than today's motorist in Airdrie.

11

A Glasgow Corporation tram heads back towards the city sometime in the late 1930s. In this period Airdrie had one of the worst unemployment rates anywhere in the British Isles. The decline of the Lanarkshire coalfield and of the iron and steel works in the vicinity of the town during the Great Depression were to blame for the drastic downturn in the fortunes of many of the locals. Employment was to be but a dream for many until the beginning of the Second World War.

In an effort to encourage people to shop locally, the town's businesses held shopping weeks. Great emphasis was made on keeping what money there was in the local area. There were competitions running in each shop and the owners all clubbed together to pay for advertising and for bunting and flags to decorate the streets. This picture shows Inglis' shop in 23-27 Stirling Street decorated for a shopping week sometime in the 1930s.

Airdrie and Coatbridge trams first ran in February 1904. The tram route was from Bank Street, Coatbridge to the terminus at Motherwell Street. The first trams arrived by rail at the North British Railway Goods Station in January 1904. This picture shows the first of these trams to run in the town. The cars could accommodate 56 passengers and over 9,500 people used the twelve trams on the first day of operation.

In January 1922, Glasgow Corporation Tramways bought the Airdrie & Coatbridge Tramways. One of the consequences of this was that the extension from Coatbridge to Baillieston was constructed. A 2d ticket would get you from Ferguslie Mills in Paisley to the terminus in Airdrie on a single tram. This is a Coronation tramcar of a type first introduced in 1936.

GRAHAM STREET LOOKING EAST FROM CROSS, AIRDRIE   A.6288.

The main reason for the decline of the trams was the appearance of considerable numbers of buses on the streets of Airdrie and Coatbridge. Their appeal was that they were able to serve many places which had no tram or train service. The bus station in Airdrie was at the New Cross. In this view, from the 1940s, there are five buses and no trams visible. Scottish Omnibuses provided a 45 minute service to Glasgow (costing 1/10d) while Alexander's Bluebird coaches provided an hourly service to Falkirk from Gartlea Bus Station.

16

THE CROSS, AIRDRIE.

B.3266.

As well as the services provided by the larger companies, there were also local companies providing services. In this view, a Baxter's bus can be seen heading off down Stirling Street. Their garage was in Gartlea Road. Services from Gartlea Bus Station included Greenshield's to Chapelhall and Irvine's to Harthill and Shotts. In the picture a large queue wait at the bus shelters outside the Royal Hotel. Even then the buses were always going in the wrong direction!

Broomknoll Parish Church dominates this 1905 view of Broomknoll Street. Opposite it, on the right, is the old Airdrie Working Men's Club. It was founded in 1869 and owed its early success to H.C. Deedes. The club was originally based in the High Street but moved to Broomknoll Street in 1885. It was extended in 1909-10 and the building demolished. A new club was then built on the site. Next door is now Lodge St. John 166. Next to the Lodge is the Housing Department in offices originally used by the Airdrie Water Board.

An Albion lorry is delivering what looks like crates of lemonade into one of the shops at the top of Broomknoll Street. Behind it, a policeman is on points duty at the Cross. An unusual feature can be seen at the back of the Little Duchess Cafe. What looks like a tower is actually a turnpike stair which dates this building to about the turn of the Nineteenth Century. This feature is now almost totally hidden from sight by the second storey that has been added to the shops along Broomknoll Street. Traffic lights first appeared at the Cross sometime in the late 1930s. At the bottom of Broomknoll Street was Airdrie's only purpose built cinema (the New Cinema) now demolished.

There have been many changes at the Cross in the last ninety years. The Central Cafe gave way in the 1930s to Airdrie Radio Service and in the 1960s, Bairds built their new shop there. Opposite was James Perman's Tailors. Before being a tailors shop, this building was used as a pub, as a jewellers (Wilkins) and as a music shop (McGlure's). The Royal Buildings were originally the Royal Hotel and, before that, the Airdrie Inn.

THE CROSS AND BANK STREET, AIRDRIE

D 6437

Most of the changes at the Cross have, however, taken place in the last thirty years. Re-development has taken place and some well known buildings were lost in the process. Subsidence from the many mines under the town was too much for the Royal Buildings and they became severely structurally weakened. After being hurriedly evacuated, they were demolished in 1969. Nowadays a concrete box which houses the Job Centre has replaced them.

Municipal Buildings, Airdrie.

Left: Construction of the Town House began in 1824 and work was completed two years later. The Town House has seen various uses over the years including being pressed into service as a hospital in 1832, as a billet for soldiers in 1837, as a court room and as a library. In 1953 the Town Clock was so worn out that it almost fell from its mountings and a new clock replaced it in 1954.

Right: When Airdrie became a Burgh in 1821, one of the responsibilities was to provide street lighting. As a result, the Airdrie Gas Light Co. was formed in 1830 and built a gasworks off Mill Street. Gas production was originally from coal mined in the local area. Some of this coal probably came from the Fruitfield Pit which was only about 100 feet away. The Burgh bought the gasworks in 1904 and expanded it on numerous occasions. The Gas Department's motto was 'Gas works for you'. The works eventually passed into the control of the Gas Board and nowadays there is no coke for sale to local businesses as all our gas comes from the North Sea.

THE TOWN CROSS, AIRDRIE.   A.6283.

Airdrie's County Buildings were completed in 1858 and burned down in November of that year. They were rebuilt and re-opened eight months later. They provided both Sheriff and J.P. Courts. The County Buildings met the same fate as befell the Royal Buildings. Undermined by subsidence, they were shored up for a number of years but eventually succumbed to the bulldozers in 1969. After being left as a gap site for some years, a new pink granite and glass creation has replaced them. Next door is, at the time of writing, being re-developed and new retail units being built.

South Bridge Street is named after the South burn which is culverted under here. This view looks uphill to the Old Cross. The Corner building at Mill Street is now Burton's the Tailors but was, at one time a branch of Claude Alexander, a Glasgow tailor. Just up from there was the Royal Cafe. The Royal was owned by Rossi and was two doors down from the old Boots the Chemist. Just to the right, behind what is now Burton's, was the Hallcraig Station. It was built in 1856, although there had been a station building there beforehand. It was originally used for both passengers and goods traffic, but after the opening of Airdrie South in the 1860s it fell into disuse as a passenger terminus.

SOUTH BRIDGE STREET, AIRDRIE.

A.4119.

Going by the clock on Dickson & Kelly's Butchers Shop, this is rush hour in South Bridge Street. Nowadays, with delivery vehicles and cars jostling for parking spaces, the street is a nightmare for the poor pedestrian. This view dates from the late 1930s.

East High Street, Airdrie.

The picture postcard this view is taken from was probably purchased in the newsagents behind the horse and cart. These buildings have now gone and the road widened at this point. The Glenkyle Bar now sits here. The bus is an early Albion, constructed in Glasgow. Albions were famous the world over for their rugged reliability and many of their lorries and buses are still around to testify to their motto of 'Sure as the Sunrise'.

The Old Cross circa 1905. The men are congregating round the old drinking fountain. This was donated to the town, along with another at the New Cross, by Provost Forrester and Laird Rankin of Auchengray in 1865. Both fountains were of cast iron and were removed at the beginning of this century. The Old Cross Bar was just one of many pubs that the town had earlier this century.

Slum clearance has helped make this scene almost unrecognisable today. Between the wars a great effort was made to remove Airdrie's bad housing. Although the town's population had been growing, little new building had actually taken place, leading to a host of problems including overcrowding, dirt and disease. The tenements further down the street would have had, at most, two or three rooms. In those two rooms there would have been box beds in the kitchen, a stove made at Steins or Smith & Wellstood's in Bonnybridge or Carron in Falkirk, and, perhaps, a dresser with the best china in the parlour. There was an outside toilet and lighting was provided by gas lamps.

Henry Scott's garage was on the right and is now under the imposing glass showroom windows of Lex Vauxhall. In 1936, Scott's were a Singer garage. A Singer Bantam could be had for £120 and Scott's could provide any model of car you desired. At the turn of the century, open air religious meetings were held on Sundays at the Old Cross.

North Bridge Street, Airdrie.

In the background, on the right, is the old Airdrie Academy. It opened in August 1895 on the grounds of Mavisbank and was a replacement for the Alexandra School. Most of the schools in the Airdrie of today are modern, having been built in the last thirty years.

The coming of the railways saw a great change take place in the town. The first railway lines were no more than waggonways. They had cast iron rails and the small waggons were hauled by horses. The first lines came to the town in the mid 1820s and included the Monkland & Kirkintilloch Railway and the Ballochney Railway. The latter railway company built a station at Commonhead and its line ran under the bridge at the bottom of the street. The Ballochney Railway originally used horse power. One horse was capable of pulling two or three waggons but the steep inclines of the railway necessitated the use of an inclined plane. There was one at Commonhead and when the horse reached it, it would be placed in a specially built waggon at the rear of its train. The train was then rolled down the incline and the horse was fed and watered before setting off again.

Many of the buildings on the west side of Commonhead have long gone. The ones this side of the railway have gone to make way for a yard used by a car rental firm and these three weavers cottages on the left have also been demolished. Today the only weavers cottages left in Airdrie are to be found at the top of the Wellwynd and have been converted into a typical weaver's cottage of the 1800s. They are well worth a visit.

Arranview is just one of the many villas that were built in and around Airdrie from the 1850s onwards. The town had a distinct advantage over Coatbridge in that it was at a higher altitude so that Airdrie managed to escape the perpetual smoke and dust that was associated with its neighbour's ironworks and associated industries.

Arranview was built in 1867 and was designed by Alexander 'Greek' Thomson, one of Scotland's greatest architects. After the Second World War, it became a children's home for a period from March 1950, its twelve rooms accommodating twenty three children. It was, like many of Thomson's works, allowed to deteriorate in the 1960s and 70s and its interior was largely lost. In 1987 it was converted into flats and the gardens built over.

Can you recognise yourself or your parents/grandparents in this picture? I acquired it a number of years ago and was told that it had been taken in Airdrie. But where? If you recognise this view or, indeed, the background, I'd love to hear from you. I think it is somewhere off the High Street and is of 1930s vintage.

Situated just next to Central Park, this view shows Parkhead Street. Apart from the church, little remains to place this scene. Wholesale demolition took place here after the Second World War and all of these houses have been replaced by blocks of flats.

AIRDRIEONIANS F.C.

The 1904-5 Airdrieonian team. Football had been played in the town from the 1860s onwards but Airdrieonians did not come into being until 1878. They were a second rate club until the mid 1880s when they started to play bigger teams. In 1886 they reached the County Final against Cambuslang. Although they were leading 3-1 the match was abandoned in the dying minutes due to a pitch invasion. A replay was organised at Hampden where Airdrieonians thrashed their opposition 5-1. The team's greatest moment was in 1924 when the Scottish Cup was brought to Airdrie. The team at that time was unbeatable and included some of the most famous names in Scottish football at the time. Hughie Gallagher had been signed for the club in 1921 and proved his worth many a time for the team. Other members of that cup winning team included Willie Russell and Bob McPhail.

36

Back row: McAuley, McLay, Wardrope, A.D. Walker (Secretary), Davidson, Rombach, Duncan, Stewart, G. Carrol (Trainer).
Front Row: Nicholl, Donaldson, Thomson, McGran, Webb, Young.

In the final, it was two goals from Russell that clinched the match against Hibs. Airdrieonians had a difficult time reaching the final though as the fourth round tie against Ayr United involved over seven hours play before the decider. Four matches, two involving extra time, were played before Airdrie scored the winning goal at Ibrox. In the semis they met Falkirk and the rest is history. The team never did manage the double but came second in the League to Rangers for three years running over the same period.

As well as the numerous railway companies that operated in and around Airdrie, there were also private operators. Some of them, like Bairds of Gartsherrie, ran on main lines with the permission of the railway companies. Others, like this locomotive, ran on internal works lines only, Shanks & McEwan had the large quarry at Whinhill and this little 0-4-0 saddle tank hauled waggons around inside the quarry. Prior to this it worked at the Etna Iron & Steel Co's works in Motherwell. It was acquired by Shanks & McEwan in 1915 and they used it until 1951 when it was scrapped and the quarry's output was shifted by road.

This was Lorry No.11 of Taylor's fleet sometime about 1912. The Bakery was just off Black Street almost opposite the police station. At the turn of the century, they were one of the largest bakers in the area. The lorry is chain driven and this load would have kept its top speed to about fifteen miles an hour. It would have been a rough journey with those solid tyres, but the driver could warn of his approach using his bulb horn. The lights were acetylene powered and were absolutely useless at night. What a difference from our modern delivery vehicles.

Chapel Street Airdrie

Chapel Street is named after the Chapel of Ease which stood part way along next to the graveyard, which is now a grassy area next to the flats. Along Chapel Street were many of the engineering firms that made the town famous including John Martin's Iron Foundry, the Airdrie Light Engineering Works & Bakery Machine Repairers and Shields & McNichol who were boilermakers.

The Airdrie Engine Works belonged to Dick & Stevenson and they manufactured colliery winding engines, stationary engines and locomotives. The railway locomotives were, when completed, steamed down Bell Street, Stirling Street and then on to the railway at Airdrie South Station. This billhead relates to the supply of a steam hammer to the Dalziell Steelworks of David Colville.

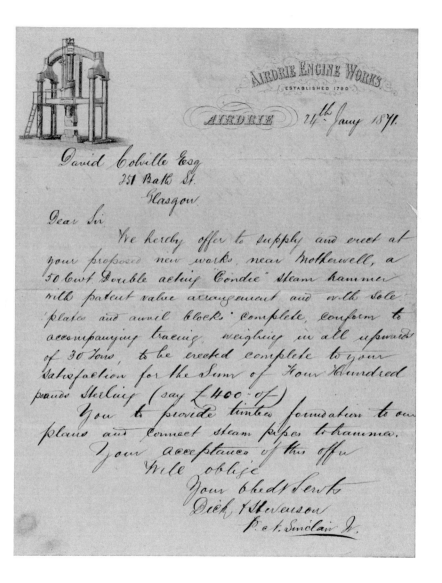

BOWLING GREEN
AND TENNIS COURT

AIRDRIE

Springwells Bowling Club green about 1912. This was just one of the bowling greens to be found in Airdrie about ninety years ago. A bowling club was established in 1852 and the sport had been played in the town for years previous to this.

When the boundaries of Airdrie were extended in 1885, Rawyards and Clarkston became part of the town. This view of Holehills has changed considerably in the ninety years since the picture was taken. Surprisingly, all of these buildings are still standing, but the area around them was developed for housing in the 1960s. Ever since the construction of Cumbernauld New Town, the A73 has become more important and, as a consequence, busier.

The message on the back of the postcard (which was sent to India in 1910) reads 'Having a fine holiday here in Airdrie'.

Motherwell Street was named after the Motherwell family who owned this area of the town. The view is looking from its junction with Black Street and Airdriehill Street. Aitken's Rawyards Tavern has gone as have all the other buildings. Rawyards was originally a small mining settlement and there were a few pits in this area, but Boots Factory is now the main employer in Rawyards.

Drumgelloch, Clarkston, Airdrie

Drumgelloch was another small mining settlement. Like many of the smaller settlements around the town, it sprang up beside a small colliery. As well as a few rows of single storey terraced miners cottages, there was the ubiquitous pub or two. The one in this view, the Drumgelloch, still survives to this day but it is the only building still standing in the row on the left.

Taken from Connor Street, this view shows a bygone Clarkston. A need for new houses in the 1950s and 60s led to the demolition of almost every building visible here. Only the building which houses the chippie remains to locate the scene.

Some of the miners rows are visible at the far right in this scene of Clarkston taken from Towers Road. Life for the miner and his family was hard. They lived in a single end and, until early this century, had no running water. Cooking was done over a coal fire and the toilet was outside. Life underground was harder still. Everything was done by hand as coal cutting machinery hadn't been invented and water would run down the seams onto the miners. In some seams, only a few feet thick, the miners would spend nine or ten hours crouching or lying on their sides picking away at the coal while the water sloshed around them. Accidents were frequent and the work hard. By the 1920s mining was dying a slow painful death and less than thirty years later, little remained except for the pit bings and derelict land around the pit heads.

Clarkston Station
and Hospital Entrance

This station was on the Airdrie-Ratho line which opened in stages from 1849 till 1872. The section from beyond Plains to Coatbridge opened in August 1862. The main stations on the line were at Bathgate, Airdrie and Coatbridge. Clarkston Station closed in 1956, but the line was still used for coal traffic and the occasional summer service until 1960. The line then terminated at Airdrie until only a few years ago when a new station was opened at Drumgelloch. Today the site of Clarkston Railway Station is used for an electricity sub-station.

BRIDGE AT
NEW MONKLAND GLEN
NEAR AIRDRIE.

BRANDON SERIES.

P.S.A. Meetings were held on many Sundays during the summer in Monkland Glen. Then, it was one of the favourite spots for a stroll by the banks of the river. Today, Monkland Glen is still sylvan, but has become overgrown and sadly neglected. The old bridge has been widened and the old mill has gone, to be replaced by housing in a style that is best termed as 'Brookside meets mock Tudor'. The tranquility of this spot is shattered by the noise of the traffic hurtling across the bridge.

FORREST STREET, AIRDRIE

Forrest Street was the terminus for the Airdrie & Coatbridge Tramways. An extension to Clarkston was amongst the proposals when the line was constructed but nothing ever came of it. Just beside the Nurses Home (built in 1904) is a horse drawn bakers van. This view dates from 1905 or 1906.

50

FORREST STREET LOOKING EAST, AIRDRIE.

This view is taken from beside the Queen Victoria Nurses Home and dates from sometime just after the end of the First World War. This side of town has more than its fair share of larger villas mainly due to the fact that the east end of Airdrie escaped from the choking fumes, dirt and noise that characterised Coatdyke and Coatbridge. Life was definitely much more sedate here.

THE CAR TERMINUS, AIRDRIE

D 6448

Most of the changes at the Car Terminus have taken place in the last thirty or forty years. It is surprising just how much the area has changed even since this photo was taken in the early 1960s. Even by then, the old ornate lamp posts had been replaced by concrete ones and a roundabout put in at the busy junction. The islands have now gone, as has the diced bonnet barrier from the roundabout itself.

Clark Street from the railway bridge circa 1916. The railway was the Newhouse to Airdrie branch of the Caledonian Railway. It was built in the 1880s and opened for traffic in July 1888. The line was built by the Caledonian Railway to access this part of North Lanarkshire. Most of the railways in this area already belonged to their arch rivals, the North British Railway, and the Caley wanted some of the traffic for themselves. As a result, this and many other lines were built purely to steal traffic from the NBR. So, when traffic levels fell, these lines were the first to go. A costly way of gaining traffic! The line closed to passengers in December 1930, but goods traffic justified the line's survival until the 1960s. The bridge is now gone and the gap sites created have since been built on.

Graham Street, Airdrie

Airdrie's Pavilion Cinema was located down on the left, past where the Community Centre is today. The pavilion was built as a roller skating rink about 1910 but that craze soon died off. Only three or four years later it was converted into a cinema which lasted well into the 1950s. Television, however, killed off the cinema. In 1952 Kirk o' Shotts transmitter opened and from then on TV started its gradual infiltration of almost every household. The 1953 Coronation gave it a big boost and in many households, ours included, a TV was rented specially for this event.

CAIRNHILL ROAD, AIRDRIE.

Cairnhill Road was laid out in the mid 1850s and since then has attracted various light industrial firms. In the old wire rope works, Marshall s grew mushrooms unsuccessfully. In 1938 Crimpy Crisps started manufacturing potato crisps there and this enterprise lasted till 1969 when a fire gutted the building. Perhaps the biggest chip pan fire ever in the history of the town!

Airdrie's Sewage Works sometime after 1935. Definitely not one of your 'Wish you were here' postcards this but it was sent through the post in 1958. The sewage works were expanded in 1935 (they had been built in 1928) and still cover a large part of the land on the other side of the railway from Rochsolloch Iron Works. As the town was expanded and many new houses were built, the Sewage Works were constructed to cope with all those flushable toilets in the inter-war council housing. This view shows the Simplex Sludge Plant.